Tasi,
The Lighthouse Dog

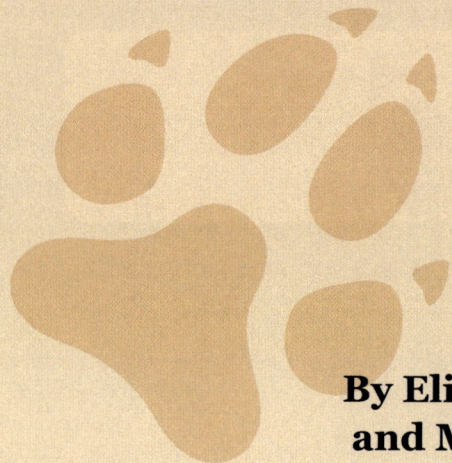

**By Elisabeth Redon
and Mark Hancock**

*Illustrations by
Adriane Bosworth*

*Photos by
Mark Hancock*

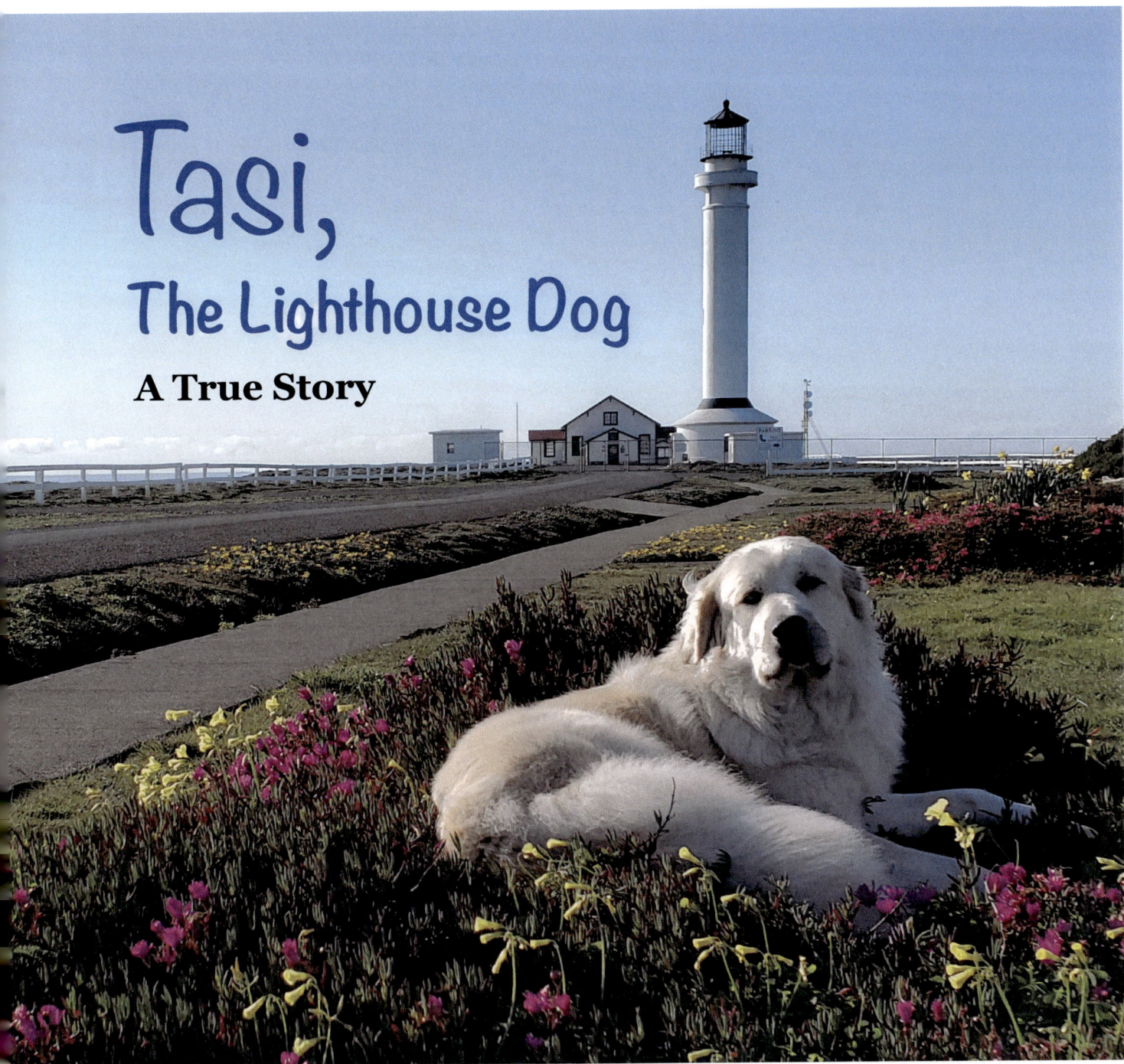

Tasi,
The Lighthouse Dog

A True Story

On a small side road off Highway 1 on the north coast of California the driver of a mini-van suddenly pulled over. She had seen a big blonde dog slowly walking along the side of the road with its head down.

When she moved closer she saw that this dog seemed to be neglected. The dog looked up at the lady with sad, sunken brown eyes. The woman noticed that it was extremely skinny, had matted fur, and big sores on its back.

She immediately went back to her minivan and made room for the dog to get inside. The driver knew she must somehow help this poor dog. She struggled as she tried to lift this enormous animal into the back of her minivan. However, this thin, sad, lonesome dog willingly climbed into the car with just a little help from the kind woman.

Understanding that the dog was probably hungry, the woman stopped at the local supermarket. She bought a whole roasted chicken without knowing it might not be the best meal for a dog. She fed it to the starving animal.

The woman wanted to keep this poor dog but knew she could not afford it. Her heart was broken, but immediate help was needed so she took the dog to the Redwood Coast Humane Society (RCHS).

The woman dropped the dog off at the RCHS where the volunteers identified her as a female Great Pyrenees. They made her comfortable in one of their kennels.

Over the next week
they took her to the
veterinarian. The vet
shaved her back, treated
her sores, fleas and ticks,
and helped her to feel
better.

This dog needed lots of "people love" so Kim, one of the RCHS volunteers, took her home. After a month of healing, she was healthy and ready to be adopted.

Kim worked with a friend named Laverne. Kim knew that her friend was looking for a dog to adopt. Since Kim was fostering this dog, Laverne went to Kim's house after work one night. When Laverne sat down, the dog ambled over to her and immediately put her front paws on Laverne's lap. Laverne was instantly in love.

Laverne's husband, Mark, had to agree to this addition to their family. Two nights later, he met this wonderful dog. As he sat on the couch, the dog jumped up next to him and put her nose right next to his ear. Mark was sure he heard her say "take me home." Guess what happened next? They adopted her and the dog was so happy. She wagged her tail and showed affection toward her new parents when they took her home.

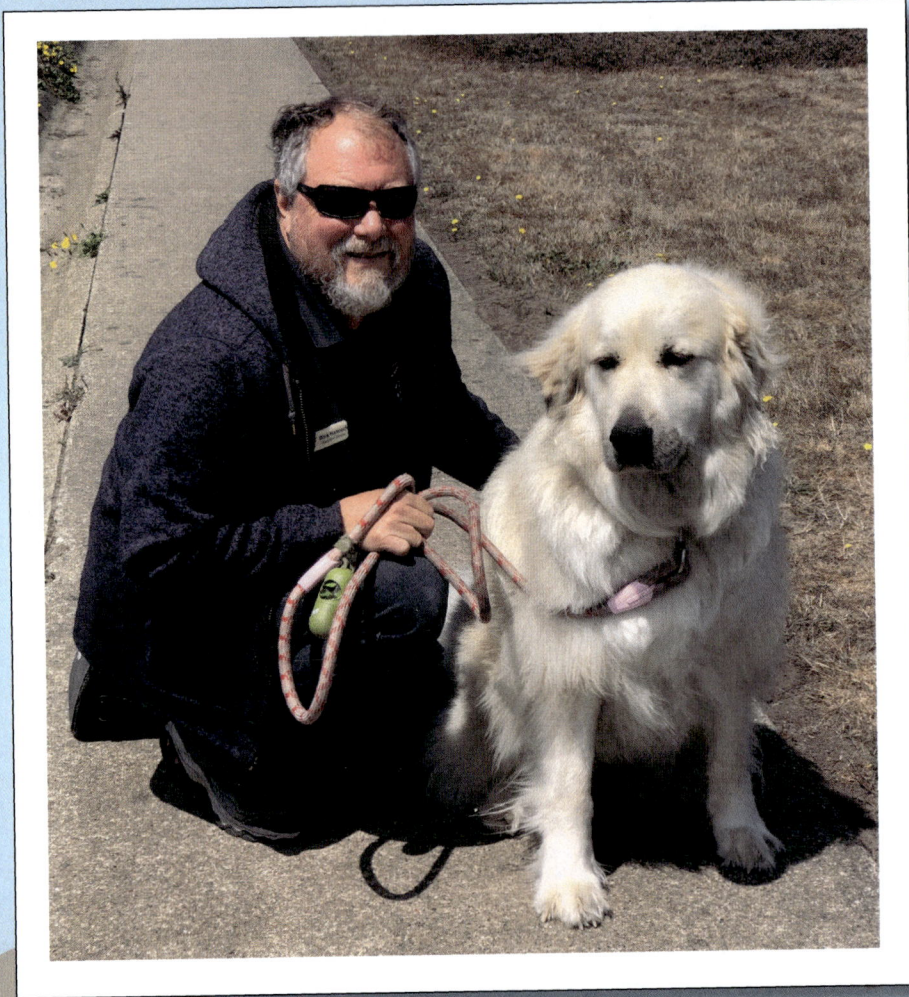

Now she was in for a big surprise. Mark is the Executive Director at the Point Arena Lighthouse. That is how the new life for this magnificent dog begins. There are 23 acres for her to roam and many visitors to greet. This dog comes to work with Mark every day as a "Lighthouse Guest Relations Manager."

She loves her surroundings as well as all the visitors who come and give her much attention. On one occasion, some very young school children came on a field trip to learn about the Lighthouse. When they entered the Fog Signal Building a little boy said to another classmate "Look at that beautiful dog!" The little girl replied "That's not a dog, that's a polar bear!"

But wait! They needed to give a name to this happy new addition to the Lighthouse family. Since Laverne's heritage is from the island of Guam, they decided that the dog should have a name from Guam. The traditional language of Guam is Chamorro and they chose "Tasi" (Tah -See) which means "ocean."

There was still one problem! There was already a gray and white cat named Arena Mina who had been the "Lighthouse Guest Relations Manager" for two years. She considered herself to be the star of the Lighthouse.

Eventually, they both learned to share the love from the many Lighthouse visitors. Now they each have a very important position: Mina the Lighthouse Cat and Tasi the Lighthouse Dog. They even have their own stickers and stuffed animals in the Light Station Store.

Tasi is a gentle giant who brings happiness and smiles to all who meet her. Tasi and Mina are the furry ambassadors as well as "Guest Relations Managers" of the Point Arena Lighthouse.

The Point Arena Lighthouse

The Point Arena Lighthouse is surrounded by water on three sides. It is a very popular visitor destination in Mendocino County. It is located at 45500 Lighthouse Road in Point Arena, California, a beautiful coastal drive 130 miles north of San Francisco.

Entrance

Tower

Fog Signal Building Museum
& Light Station Store

Lodging

Water Tank

From Mark Hancock

This book is dedicated to the wonderful volunteers at Redwood Coast Humane Society. Their caring, no kill shelter refuses no animal and they work tirelessly to get all their pets adopted to caring, loving homes. Special thanks to Tasi's "first Mom and Dad" Kim and Brian Park for fostering Tasi to health and bringing her, Laverne and me together – I am so grateful to them for bringing Tasi into my life.

From Elisabeth Redon

With heartfelt gratitude to my illustrator, Adriane Bosworth.

With heartfelt gratitude to my co-author/editor, Mark Hancock.

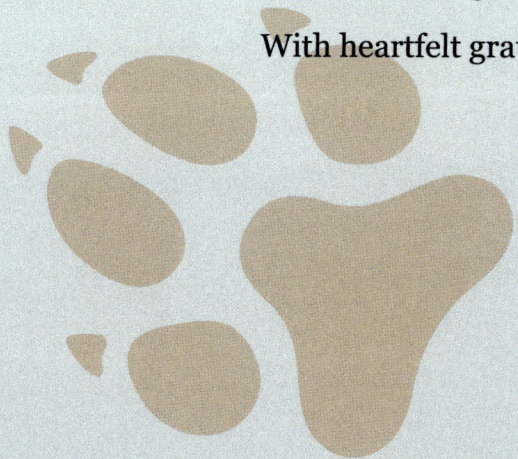

Come visit
Tasi and Mina
at the
Point Arena Lighthouse
where they will welcome
your affection!

Made in the USA
Middletown, DE
23 January 2024